Terms and Conditions

LEGAL NOTICE

The Publisher has strived to be as accurate and complete as possible in the creation of this report, notwithstanding the fact that he does not warrant or represent at any time that the contents within are accurate due to the rapidly changing nature of the Internet.

While all attempts have been made to verify information provided in this publication, the Publisher assumes no responsibility for errors, omissions, or contrary interpretation of the subject matter herein. Any perceived slights of specific persons, peoples, or organizations are unintentional.

In practical advice books, like anything else in life, there are no guarantees of income made. Readers are cautioned to reply on their own judgment about their individual circumstances to act accordingly.

This book is not intended for use as a source of legal, business, accounting or financial advice. All readers are advised to seek services of competent professionals in legal, business, accounting and finance fields.

You are encouraged to print this book for easy reading.

Table Of Contents

Introduction

The term "monetization" now has a new connotation. People are trying to make money off of pretty much anything and everything in these challenging times. Some people are having great success, generating various revenue streams from a single product. While others simply pass the time, unable to really grasp the idea of monetization.

Here is an eBook that explains how to monetize your content. How to increase your income with little work while ensuring that it continues to flow into your bank account?

Summary

How do you monetize? How do individuals approach it??

- 6 -

The Name of the Game

There are numerous meanings of "monetization" that you may find online if you do some research on the subject. Actually, the term "monetization" refers to a wide range of diverse activities, but in a more general sense, we may say that it refers to earning money through activities that most people wouldn't typically consider to be profitable. You have monetized the collection, for instance, if you are able to sell your dad's or your uncle's old collection of Archie's Comics for a healthy money.

Monetization is the process of generating income from commonplace items in novel ways.

It is fairly simple to understand why people are going all out in an effort to profit from everything that comes to mind. or perhaps hidden from view. People can earn money by using their unique talents. You are monetizing your talent if you have a special knack for arithmetic and use it to tutor the next-door neighbor's child. You are monetizing your writing talent if you create material and sell it to a customer.

Although we are all quite aware of monetizing, it's unlikely that we've ever done it systematically. Our jobs provide us with a living, and we often accept the money we receive without trying to push our luck too far. It is crucial to realize that there are numerous additional opportunities for profit, nevertheless. If we play our cards right, we can create streams of passive income from setups we make once and profit from the inflow of cash for the rest of our lives. Similar to royalties on your stuff, that would be.

What you can monetize is what you can earn money from in addition to your primary occupation. It's about your effort, not how valuable the final result is. It involves realizing that a certain skill or ability may be made money, and then figuring out how to do it.

Here, we'll look at a variety of strategies for creating sources of revenue for yourself out of things you would not have thought would be profitable.

Summary

It may sound hopeless, but it's true. Rich folks didn't become that way by sabotaging opportunities.

Making Money Out of Anything... *Anything!*

You can earn money out of anything, which is the first thing you need to understand if you want to gain the courage to do it.

But what exactly are we talking about when we say "anything"? It might be something you've created. You can make money off of something if it has a use, and occasionally even if it doesn't. Or, it can be something you obtained from someone else and are now permitted to sell for a profit. Or it can be a skill you possess. It can just be your general knowledge or specific expertise about a certain topic.

Even those who feel as though they have nothing have a lot of stuff that they can sell to get money. There is no squandering of space here.

Let's talk about something very, very positive before diving right into discussions about how you can do this. The principle of attraction. This legislation has taken the world by storm and is incredibly relevant to the subject of our conversation. In a word, the law states that when you strongly desire something, the entire universe will conspire to grant your wish. The law does indeed indicate that thoughts have consequences. It refers to the power of the mind's energy, which truly causes events to occur.

This is a very real law, and those who have claimed that it is absurd and doesn't apply to them initially expressed their lack of confidence in it. You must have complete faith in the law for it to function. Just concentrate on your goal. Consider what you desire. Think without hesitation or flinching. Things will start to happen gradually. You are forced to act in that path when you think that profoundly. Your only focus will be on obtaining that one objective. Naturally, everything will begin to fall into place. Your unrelenting focus on your deepest desires will help you get there.

You must adhere to this rule even if you have plans to monetize your work. You must never, ever believe that there is no money to be made from this. In fact, consider the bigger picture rather than just the financial aspect. As an aside, the money is received. When you work hard, you'll eventually be paid for your efforts regardless of how long it takes.

Summary

The real money is being made on the Internet.

Why You Just Cannot Forget the Internet

Today, monetization is practically a given for online enterprises. The Internet will be the first and most important area of action for everyone looking to generate money from anything. They use online resources for monetization for a variety of reasons.

First and foremost, today's monetization paradigm is entirely different. Conventional thinking is no longer prevalent. They are putting their thoughts to work and trying to generate money off of fresh concepts and ideas. This is impossible unless the business owners can track down individuals who are interested in what they are selling. Simply said, they need to identify individuals who they can consider their niche clients because they are working in specialized areas.

The Internet makes that possible. There are a ton of ways to locate individuals interested in whatever it is that you are attempting to do when you are working on the Internet. You want to create a fan site for a programmer that nobody else in your area watches. You can carry out that action online. You wish to discuss a pastime that you believe no one else has. You'll be shocked to learn just how many individuals on the Internet appreciate you in particular. Do you possess a talent that you believe no one else values? You can find a huge number of people who do on the Internet. Or perhaps you created a product that nobody else in your vicinity finds beneficial. You'll be pleasantly delighted to learn that there is an online niche market for that goods as well.

The Internet helps you feel more confident, and that's what matters most. You feel more confident about creating that product or conceptualizing that idea and generating revenue when you are aware that many other people share your interests and are also interested in what you are trying to offer.

The fact that there is no rejection is its best feature. Today, you may attract prospective buyers to your door with the aid of the Internet, a far cry from the days when dealers had to hawk their items to consumers. Internet marketing is a great option if you are a shy, introverted person who cringes at the thought of rejection.

The main lure, of course, is the vast array of resources available online. There are strategies you may use to attract customers who are queuing outside your door to purchase whatever it is you are selling. Even if it doesn't do anything else for you, this is what gives you more self-assurance and motivates you to keep working on your business.

Summary

The first thing you need do is create something well-known that you can use as a means of earning money.

Build Something Successful

The numerous fan sites that American Idol has produced are well-known to almost all of its fans. Most of these websites began as simple fan sites with no consideration for money, but as they gained incredible popularity, their creators began to wonder if they would be able to monetize them as well. As a result, a sizable monetization option emerged.

The Harry Potter series experienced the same thing. One of the almost-official Harry Potter fan sites, Mugglenet.com, didn't start out as a business. It was merely a gathering spot for fans of the child wizard to gather and learn more about him. But after that, it became incredibly popular, and who wouldn't consider making money from it?

In both of these instances, people developed the things in question without ever considering the possibility of making money off of them. This implies that you are truly not required to produce something with money in the picture from the very beginning. You might even return later and sell what you still have. To monetize a product, you only need to make it incredibly popular.

Making anything incredibly popular on the Internet is a remarkably simple process. You are able to use blogs as a tool. Create a blog using Wordpress.com or Blogger.com, both of which offer free blogging tools, and then get popularity for it. Your blog can be made profitable in a variety of ways after it gains popularity (i.e., a large following), for as by selling eBooks, email subscriptions, or possibly even a membership site in the future. Even if you don't want to go all in, i.e. establish a blog right away, you can still look into revenue streams using tools like social networking. Create communities, invite people to them, and provide them with valuable content to increase the popularity of your business (it's time we starting calling this a business). As more individuals arrive, you'll see that you have more opportunities to make money.

Summary

Your journey toward monetization has already begun. You now require clients who will pay you money.!

Goodwill Hunting and Finding Niches

It will be incredibly difficult to monetize anything if you don't target the proper audience. If you can't find individuals willing to pay money to learn your recipes from you, how can you expect to make money off of them? You understand the necessity of locating your specialty.

SEO, or search engine optimization, is one of the greatest ways to accomplish that on the Internet. If you are experimenting with online enterprises, chances are good that you already have some basic knowledge of SEO. What it signifies if you don't is as follows. Simply put, SEO refers to optimizing your website (a blog counts as a website, too) for search engines. This is quite significant since search engines are where people go when they want to get information. When looking for information, people usually type a term or phrase into a search engine like Google, Yahoo!, or Ask. They then click the links that appear. Most of the time, people just click on the links on the first page, and very few even visit the second. Therefore, appearing on the first page of any search engine becomes crucial for anyone wishing to achieve Internet fame (and subsequently monetize their efforts).

Even if you don't have your own websites, you can build up a sizable fan base by posting on other people's blogs and forums. Many blog commenters receive a lot of feedback, which helps them grow their own fan bases. As soon as they amass such a following, they immediately start creating their own blogs or websites and introducing these people to them. Without making any financial commitment on your part, this might be an excellent strategy to discover your niche and build trust with them as well.

The use of article marketing is another strategy. You might publish articles on the topic you're attempting to monetize. After that, these articles could be published on websites like EzineArticles.com, iSnare.com, ArticleAlley.com, GoArticles.com, ArticleCity.com, etc. The fact that these sites are already well-liked by search engines is the strongest reason to submit your articles there. Consequently, if you were to submit some really educational pieces here, you may garner a sizable fan base for them. Additionally, bear in mind that readers who find your content will be those who are truly looking for knowledge in that particular field.

Chapter 6:

Summary

Only when you are sure in what you are selling can you begin to monetize. Even a fruit vendor needs to be persuaded that his oranges are excellent or no one will buy them from him. However, you will undoubtedly play for higher stakes than just a few oranges here.

Promoting Your Stuff Online – When Does the Confidence Come?

Confidence is one of the key ingredients needed to sell anything. You are truly seeking for it. However, when does the assurance arrive?

Your confidence might be apparent immediately away. You can think quite optimistically that you can make money out of a certain short story you've written or a film you've made demonstrating a specific method for making bouillabaisse. You certainly can; there are various ways to do it. There is still a long way to go, but this is the beginning of confidence.

You need to understand that early confidence does not last in this situation. The most crucial thing is that you must build up your confidence. It has to be strengthened. What else boosts your confidence? Results matter most.

Your confidence starts to grow when you realize that things are truly going the way you want them to go and that you are actually getting the money you set out to get.

However, it's not just about the cash. Any kind of result could be helpful in keeping you going. Some people may find encouragement to keep moving forward in even the smallest comment on an article they've written or a blog post they've created. Give it a shot. Blog about a subject that is dear to your heart. If you receive a response to that, you know that at least one person was somewhat affected by what you said. It gives you the much-needed boost you need to perform better at work.

You could be motivated by anything, for any kind of outcome. It might be more people visiting your blog, more people leaving comments, more people inviting you to join a social networking group, more people emailing you, more people asking you directly about a topic in which you have knowledge, and so on. Or, maybe most significantly and eventually, it might be someone who really pays you for what you are attempting to sell.

What actually boosts your confidence is this. However, you must keep in mind that you must begin with some measure of confidence. Although it would be ideal to start out with unwavering confidence, if that doesn't seem to be the case, you can at least find inspiration in the successes that continue to come your way.

Summary

Nothing boosts an entrepreneur's self-confidence more than individuals praising their companies.

The Power of Viral Marketing

Viral marketing has always been important, but in the age of Internet marketing, it has taken on a whole new meaning. Have you ever heard from a friend that a certain book was recommended to read, and you ended up buying and reading it? Or have you ever gone to a restaurant on someone else's advice? You are already familiar with viral marketing if you have engaged in these activities. When a person spreads the word about a product to someone in their network, that is known as viral marketing.

Why is viral marketing relevant to our discussion topic? This is due to the fact that using viral marketing is the best and most efficient approach to monetize something. When someone recommends your company to someone they know, there is a lot greater likelihood that you will attract a new customer, don't you think? If someone you know uses and recommends something, don't you get more interested in it? That is how it operates for everyone.

However, the amount of business you generate is not what matters most. It is the sense of confidence it gives you. You know you are doing something right when customers go above and above to not only buy your product but also enthusiastically suggest it to others. Being the recipient of so many compliments and strong recommendations, you start to feel content and motivated to do better.

So, where can you sell your products using viral means? The greatest place to do it is unquestionably on your blog. Make consistent postings there. Visitors will come. They'll use your product to some extent. If they enjoy it, they will tell others about it. Some people may do it directly on the blog. This is great for your ego!

Use social networking websites instead. You might invite others to join a certain group on the majority of social networking sites. You might form a group for your own company. Invite people over. Everyone in the neighborhood learns about your product when some of them start using and endorsing it. The most crucial part is that you also learn about it. You start to feel very happy with how things are going. Not only is money coming in, but you have also created a huge number of satisfied customers who, you can be sure, will spread the word about your product to others.

However, the amount of business you generate is not what matters most. It is the sense of confidence it gives you. You know you are doing something right when customers go above and above to not only buy your product but also enthusiastically suggest it to others. Being the recipient of so many compliments and strong recommendations, you start to feel content and motivated to do better.

So, where can you sell your products using viral means? The greatest place to do it is unquestionably on your blog. Make consistent postings there. Visitors will come. They'll use your product to some extent. If they enjoy it, they will tell others about it. Some people may do it directly on the blog. This is great for your ego!

Use social networking websites instead. You might invite others to join a certain group on the majority of social networking sites. You might form a group for your own company. Invite people over. Everyone in the neighborhood learns about your product when some of them start using and endorsing it. The most crucial part is that you also learn about it. You start to feel very happy with how things are going. Not only is money coming in, but you have also created a huge number of satisfied customers who, you can be sure, will spread the word about your product to others.

Chapter 8:

Summary

When you have a sizable group of customers who are enthusiastic about your offering and assist you in spreading the word about it to further customers through recommendations or other means, you are fully set.

- 33 -

Building Your Battalion of Interested People

It seems sense that if you have a large army of people promoting your product of passion, you will have far greater success in making money off of it. You may accomplish this very easily using the many resources the Internet has to offer.

Keep in mind that when you are dealing with many people who share your views, confidence will naturally arise. These folks are your source of confidence; when you witness them promoting your goods, you get more motivated.

So, how do you start recruiting people to form this army? Lead generation is one strategy for doing this. Quite simply, lead generation refers to gathering contact information from those who are even slightly interested in what you are attempting to sell. There are a number of ways to go about doing this, but one of the simplest and most popular ways is to offer customers freebies like eBooks or email subscriptions. On your blog's page, you might advertise these freebies and provide a download link. However, they won't be taken straight to the giveaway page from this download URL. They will be directed to a squeeze page where their email addresses will be requested. Because they will receive anything in exchange for their email addresses, they won't mind giving them. Once you have these email addresses, you can utilize them to inform people about your company in a variety of ways.

Your responsibility is to continue giving them high-quality material once someone joins your list. It could happen that they are greatly pleased by your newsletters, eBooks, or emails and decide to purchase your offering. When they feel that way, they join your powerful battalion. They won't mind spreading the word about your product.

The same holds true when you are making money off of your material. You might ask readers to subscribe to your feeds once they finish reading your article. They will be alerted anytime you update the content as soon as they do that. They intend to return. They might join your club of appreciation. Such individuals will then advocate for you to others (you could speed that up by giving them an incentive, such as a free subscription or an eBook, etc.). Your army is at work right now. It is extending the reach of your business idea.

Summary

Never should monetization be a one-time event. It must be a sustained endeavor that can continue to provide income.

Setting Up Streams of Residual Money

If you can make money off of something once, you can make money off of it repeatedly.

This is a crucial point, and it bears even more weight online because it is actually very feasible to profit from anything multiple times.

The underlying idea behind this is residual income. Let's first define residual income. Money that keeps flowing for something you did once is known as residual income. Authors who receive royalties for their books are paid on a continuing basis. They only spent one time working on the book, and then they virtually always receive royalties from sales of it.

On the Internet, you may carry out the same actions. You could write an eBook, for instance, and advertise it on numerous websites around the Internet. This eBook might be about something you want to make money from, like your proficiency with a six-string guitar. You might produce authoritative content, share it on your blog and other affiliate websites, and then market it. Soon enough, individuals will start paying to read the eBook, and as the wave of viral marketing starts to flow, you'll start seeing more revenue created for your needs as well.

Every blog that is developed, every website that is made, and every piece of writing that is published online generates residual income. These are your digital footprints, which you can simply explore to continue making money. You must be aware of Internet marketers who have amassed millions of dollars. However, they didn't do this by working hard all the time on everything. They achieved this by making money out of their knowledge and experience. Although their efforts were one-time, they made significant marketing efforts, which helped to keep things moving.

You must therefore get out and gain as much exposure online as you can. Learn about the idea of link exchange and affiliate marketing. You can do this to disperse oneself across a bigger virtual area. This will draw more attention to what you are attempting to offer and provide you with a steady flow of income that you can be proud of.

Summary

If you aren't confident in your ability, you can't profit from the world's hottest product.

Realizing the Power of 'I Can'

Everything starts with confidence.

Even if you were given the best-selling product in the world and told to make money off of it, you couldn't accomplish so if you lacked confidence in it.

Worldwide, numerous McDonald's and Taco Bell franchises have been a failure. How come they failed? Was it as a result of the product's lack of prior validation? The sellers' lack of confidence was the real cause of the situation.

Everything you achieve comes from within. So far, we've made all the wrong decisions. We talk about being in the ideal setting at the ideal moment. That is all well and good, but how could you ever achieve in anything if you didn't seize the chance when it presented itself? Realizing and believing in our ability to accomplish is the first step toward success. We must transform the idea of decency into possibility rather than reject it.

As a result, you can profit from the slogans you can compose so effectively. The cakes you bake can bring in money for you. The knowledge you have regarding hydraulic screws can be used to generate income. Your love of Lost can be turned into cash. All you need to do is have faith in your ability to profit from these activities.

Start by imagining that there are people out there who would like or perhaps even require what it is that you are trying to sell. You gain confidence once you are certain that there is a real market. You realize that now that the necessary personnel are in place, all that is left to do is deliver the goods.

There are numerous internet methods for making genuine donations. The Internet has the power to bring this particular group 'of people' close to you. The Internet is what gives you such unwavering confidence in everything.

Explore the power of "I can" thus. It strongly encourages you to earn money.

Conclusion

If you put your mind to it, you can certainly generate money from scrap and garbage. It is also possible to continually monetize something if it has true value.

You need to start by giving yourself the belief that you can accomplish that.

Maybe that's happened by now.

All the best to you!!!